MASTERING *ORIGAMI*

ORIGAMI
VEHICLES

MASTERING *ORIGAMI*

ORIGAMI

VEHICLES

Tom Butler and Michael G. LaFosse

Enslow Publishing
101 W. 23rd Street
Suite 240
New York, NY 10011
USA
enslow.com

Published in 2017 by Enslow Publishing, LLC
101 W. 23rd Street, Suite 240, New York, NY 10011

Library of Congress Cataloging-in-Publication Data

Names: Butler, Tom.
Title: Origami vehicles / Tom Butler and Michael G. LaFosse.
Description: New York : Enslow Publishing, 2017 | Series: Mastering origami | Includes bibliographical references and index.
Identifiers: ISBN 9780766079526 (pbk.) | ISBN 9780766079533 (library bound) | ISBN 9780766079588 (6 pack)
Subjects: LCSH: Origami—Juvenile literature.
Classification: LCC TT870.B885 2017 | DDC 736'.982—dc23

Printed in the United States of America

To Our Readers: We have done our best to make sure all website addresses in this book were active and appropriate when we went to press. However, the author and the publisher have no control over and assume no liability for the material available on those websites or on any websites they may link to. Any comments or suggestions can be sent by e-mail to customerservice@enslow.com.

Photos Credits: Art throughout book: windesign/Shutterstock.com (geometric background), Janos Timea/Shutterstock.com (banners), butterflycreative/Shutterstock.com (book title); origami projects by Michael G. LaFosse; photographs of projects by Adriana Skura and Cindy Reiman.

CONTENTS

INTRODUCTION

Origami is the art of folding paper to make shapes. In the Japanese language, *ori* means "folding" and *kami* means "paper." It is an art and a craft enjoyed by people of all ages throughout the world.

Origami uses a language of symbols, just like music. Once you know origami symbols, you can read an origami book from anywhere in the world. Use the key on pages 8 and 9 to help you make your origami projects. The key explains terms such as *mountain fold* and *valley fold* and shows you the different symbols that are used throughout the book.

All of the origami projects in this book are made from square-shaped paper. Most origami paper has color on only one side, but you do not need to buy special origami paper. You can make origami using gift-wrapping paper, old magazines, colorful notepapers, and even candy wrappers! Just be sure the paper you use is square. It also must be the right size for the project you are making. When you start a project, make sure the paper faces in the same way as it does in the instructions.

Some origami projects, such as the airplane and truck in this book, need more than one sheet of

paper. These two-piece models let you mix and match different colors of paper in one model.

As you fold, look ahead at the next instruction to see what the paper's shape will look like. This will help you better understand how the symbols and drawings work together. And as you complete these projects, just remember: the most important instruction is to have fun!

ORIGAMI FOLDS AND SYMBOLS

1. MOUNTAIN FOLD

MOUNTAIN FOLD LINE

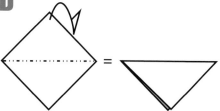

To make a mountain fold, hold the paper so the bottom (white) side is facing up. Fold the top corner back (away from you) to meet the bottom corner.

2. VALLEY FOLD

VALLEY FOLD LINE

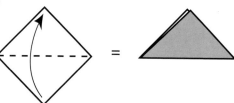

To make a valley fold, hold the paper so the white side is facing up. Fold the bottom corner up to meet the top corner.

3. ROTATE

ROTATE

6. CUT

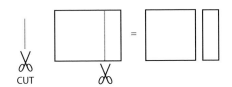

CUT

4. TURN OVER

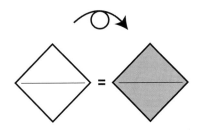

7. FOLD AND UNFOLD

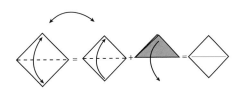

5. MOVE OR PUSH

MOVE or PUSH

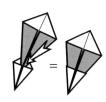

8. DIRECTION ARROW

AIRPLANE

It is fun to invent new paper airplanes. More than 150 different designs have been invented. Most of the paper airplanes that have been designed are made by folding only one piece of paper, but this two-piece design flies so well and is so simple that it may become one of your favorites.

After you have folded this airplane and flown it, you may be surprised to find that if you pull the "nose" from underneath, the airplane turns into an elephant!

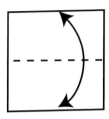

1. Use two square pieces of paper 6 inches (15.2 cm) wide or less. Smaller models fly the best. Fold one piece in half, edge to edge, and unfold.

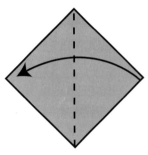

2. Fold the other piece of paper in half, corner to corner, to make a triangle.

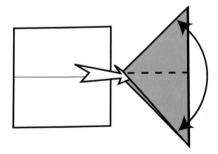

3. Fold the triangle in half, corner to corner, and unfold. Slip the other paper inside the triangle, making sure to line up the creases.

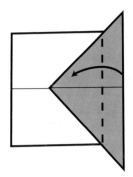

4. Fold over the long edge of the triangle.

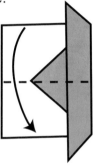

5. Fold in half, wing to wing.

6. Fold down the wings, one on each side. Open the wings and throw!

DOUBLE-FLAP PLANE

Real airplanes have flaps on their wings to make the planes move in different directions. Flaps called elevators make the plane climb or **descend**. An aileron is a flap that makes the plane **bank** for a turn. Some planes have a vertical flap called a rudder on the tail. The rudder also helps the plane turn. This paper plane has elevons on its main wings. An elevon flap combines the **functions** of an elevator and aileron. The folds for the elevons are in Step 5. As an experiment, fold one plane with elevons and one without. You will see the importance of the flaps.

1. Use printer paper that measures 8 1/2 by 11 inches (21.6 x 27.9 cm). Fold it in half lengthwise, left to right.

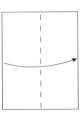

2. Valley fold the bottom corner. Take care to match it to the long, open edge on the right. Unfold and open the paper completely.

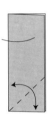

3. Do you see a triangle shape? Valley fold twice, one at a time, along the dotted lines. The folds need to be the same size. Make the first fold so that it meets the top of the wide end of the triangle shape, as shown by the dotted lines.

4. Valley fold the left and the right corners of the bottom folded edge to meet at the center crease. Unfold.

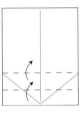

5. Mountain fold the two upper corners back. Unfold. Valley fold the bottom corners up to meet the crease lines that you made in Step 4. Unfold.

6. Tuck the bottom corners behind the folded edge of paper. Use the creases made in Steps 4 and 5.

7. Valley fold the side edges to form the fins. Unfold. Mountain fold the plane in half, wing to wing, so that the folded V-shaped layers remain on the outside.

8. Position the plane so that the nose faces left. Valley fold the wing twice on the side that is facing you, as shown. Mountain fold the wing twice on the other side.

TWO-PIECE STUNT PLANE

Origami designs made from two or more papers are called **compound** models. This origami airplane gets its name because it is made with two pieces of paper. It is called a stunt plane because it can fly through the air and do fancy loops and curvy dips. Do flying experiments with your stunt airplane. Curl up the two back corners of the wings to make your stunt airplane loop. Does it fly differently if you curl the corners just a little, or a lot, or if you curl them down instead of up? How does the plane fly when you throw it fast, or slow, or if you just let it drop? Have fun finding out!

1. Use two 8-1/2-inch- (21.6-cm) square papers. Use two different colors of paper to make your plane look especially nice. Valley fold and unfold the first paper. You have made a center crease. This will be the rear, main wing section.

2. Position the other paper so that it looks like a diamond shape. Use the dotted lines as a guide to fold from the right to the left corner. Now you have a triangle. This will be the front wing section.

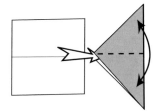

3. Fold and unfold the triangle to make a center crease. Slip the rear, main wing section completely inside the front wing section. Be sure to line up the center creases on both pieces of paper.

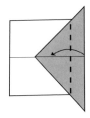

4. Look at the dotted line before you fold. Next carefully fold the wide end of the triangle along the dotted line.

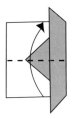

5. Valley fold the plane. Make sure you fold along the center crease line as shown by the dotted line.

6. Valley fold the side that is facing you, and mountain fold the other side. Make sure you fold so that the upper straight edge of the wings meets at the bottom edges of the plane. Open the wings straight out. You are now ready to fly your plane! Try folding up the back part of the plane wings to see it do neat loops!

SQUID PLANE

After you fold this paper plane, you will see why it is called a squid plane. The plane resembles the body of a squid! In many countries, printer paper is a little longer and narrower than the printer paper used in the United States. The paper's **proportions** make it a true rectangle. The true rectangle shape is ideal for making a squid plane. The printer paper used in the United States measures 8 1/2 by 11 inches (21.6 x 27.9 cm). The size is too big to make a perfect squid plane. The **canard wings** of a squid plane are too wide when folded from this paper. This makes the plane **stall**. However, you can correct this by adding two folds to the canard wings.

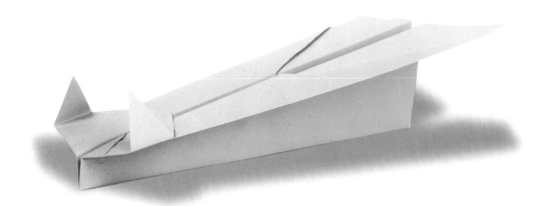

1. Use printer paper 8 1/2 by 11 inches (21.6 x 27.9 cm). Fold the paper in half lengthwise. Unfold. You have made a center crease.

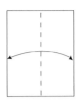

2. Carefully valley fold each of the bottom corners to meet at the center crease line.

3. Turn the paper over so the folds are facing down. The pointed part is the nose of the squid plane.

4. Valley fold the two edges on either side so that they meet at the center crease line. Look at the next step to see how it should appear.

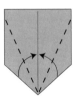

5. Pull out the two corners from behind the nose. Look at Step 6 to see how the shape should appear. Notice that the front of the plane looks diamond shaped.

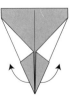

6. Valley fold the diamond shape. You have made the canard wings. Do you see the two triangles, one inside the other? Look at Step 7 for help.

7. Valley fold the two corner points of the canard wing. Use the dotted lines to help you make this fold. Next fold the paper in half, wing to wing, so that the folds are inside.

8. Valley fold the side facing you and mountain fold the other side. Make sure to match the flat wing edges to the bottom edge of the plane.

9. Open the wings and lift up the two tips of the canard wing. This is how your squid plane should appear from the back.

Back view of wings

LUCKY PLANE

This is called the lucky airplane because you can throw it into the air any which way and it will recover and land nicely and safely. The open space under the paper plane's nose can be used for special launches. Put your pointing finger inside this space and whip your arm forward to send it quickly into the air. The faster the flight, the more the plane will loop!

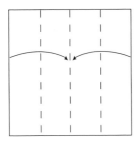

1. Use 8-inch- (20.3-cm-) square paper. Fold in half lengthwise. Unfold. Fold the outer edges to the center crease. Do not unfold.

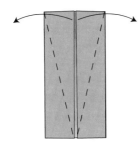

2. Use the dotted lines to help you fold in this step. Valley fold the two top inside corners outward. Look at Step 3 to see how it will appear after you fold.

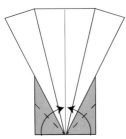

3. Valley fold the bottom corners to meet at the center crease line. Look at Step 4 to see how it should appear. Do you see a triangle shape?

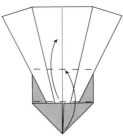

4. Valley fold the triangle shape to the base. Valley fold again to the place where the tip of the triangle touches the center line. You will see a rectangle shape.

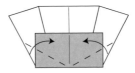

5. Valley fold the bottom two corners to make a point. Notice that their edges do not meet at the center crease line.

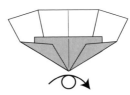

6. Turn the plane over so that all the folds face downward.

7. Valley fold the wings. Next, open up the two wings. Now your lucky plane is ready for some flying adventures!

SPACE SHUTTLE

A space shuttle rides a rocket to get above the **atmosphere** where there are no clouds or air. It is sometimes used to carry people and equipment to a space station, and sometimes to bring satellites into orbit. A space shuttle can be used to visit an orbiting telescope to service or repair it. Like a submarine, a space shuttle must hold all the food, water, and air that a crew will need. When a space shuttle lands, it glides to Earth without power. The bottom of the space shuttle gets very hot when it comes into contact with the atmosphere at high speed. The bottom is covered with special tiles that protect the shuttle from very high heat.

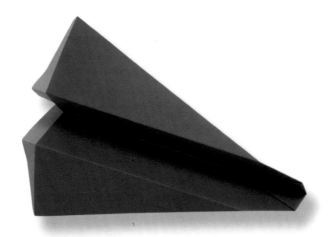

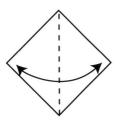

4. Fold down the top of the triangle so that it falls below the bottom edge of the paper.

1. Use a square piece of paper 10 inches (25.4 cm) wide or less. If you are using origami paper, start with the white side up. Fold the paper in half, corner to corner, then unfold it.

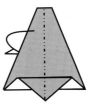

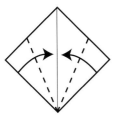

5. Fold in half, making sure that the triangle of paper is on the outside of the shape.

2. Carefully fold two edges to the crease to make a kite shape.

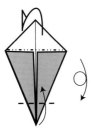

6. Pull the triangle to make it stand out like the tail of an aircraft. Press the paper hard to make it stay in place.

3. Fold up a little of the bottom corner, then fold down the top corner to the back. Turn over the paper.

7. Fold out the wings, one on each side.

TWO-PIECE JET

All the paper airplanes in this book are **gliders**. They do not have **propulsion**, which means that they do not have engines or motors. The first motorized flying machines used **propellers** to help them travel through the air. Later, the jet engine was invented. This allowed planes to travel at greater speeds. Faster planes use smaller wings, and the shape of a plane's **fuselage** allows it to fly through the air like a bullet or an arrow. This paper airplane is called a jet because of its shape. It is designed to fly straight, far, and fast. This plane is a good design to make if you want to have target competitions with your friends.

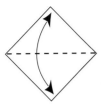

1. Use two 8-inch (20.3-cm) square papers. Position one of the papers so that it is diamond shaped. Valley fold and unfold. You have made a crease line.

2. Valley fold the top corner to the center crease line. Valley fold the bottom corner to the center line. Notice that these folds are angled.

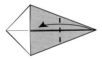

3. Fold the narrow end to the bottom edge of the triangle you created in the last step. Use the dotted line as a guide.

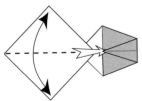

4. Valley fold the second paper and unfold. Slip the right corner of this paper inside the first paper. Be sure to line up the creases.

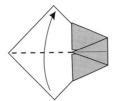

5. Valley fold in half along the center crease.

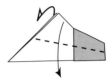

6. Valley fold the wing facing you, and mountain fold the other side. The front top edge should line up with the bottom fold.

7. Open the wings and throw the plane!

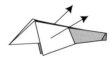

Back view of wings

8. This is how the back view of the wings should look.

TRUCK

A truck is a vehicle that is designed to carry large or heavy objects. Using trucks is an **efficient** way to move things around the country. Some trucks carry fresh food and are like refrigerators on wheels. We can have fresh fruits and vegetables even in the winter because these items are brought by truck from warmer climates to colder areas.

This origami truck is made from two pieces of paper. One piece is the vehicle, and the other piece is the load. You can change the size or color of the load. You can even write or draw on the load to show what your truck is carrying.

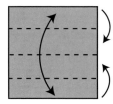

1. Use two square pieces of paper 10 inches (25.4 cm) wide or less. If you are using origami paper, start with the colored side up. Fold the first paper in half, bottom edge to top edge, and unfold. Fold the top and bottom edges to the crease.

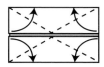

2. Fold out the four corners.

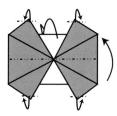

3. Fold a little of each of the four corners to the back, then mountain fold in half.

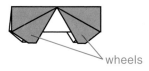

4. The paper should look like this.

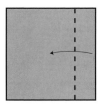

5. Fold in the right edge of the second paper.

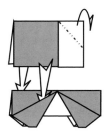

6. Mountain fold in half.

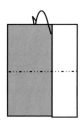

7. Fold back the right corner. Insert this second paper into the first, one edge on each side and behind the wheels.

CAR

Cars come in many shapes and sizes. There are fast cars for racing, and there are big cars that can carry many people. The word *car* is the short form of the word *carriage*. Carriages used to be pulled by horses. The first cars were called horseless carriages. Many of them were powered by electricity. Today most cars run on gasoline, which is a fuel that uses oxygen. There are also some new designs for cars powered by electricity.

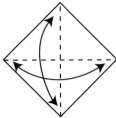

1. Use two square pieces of paper 10 inches (25.4 cm) wide or less. If you are using origami paper, start with the white side up for the first piece of paper and the colored side up for the second. Fold the first paper in half, corner to corner, both ways. Unfold each time.

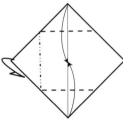

2. Fold in the top and bottom corners. Mountain fold the left corner. All three corners should touch the center creases where they cross.

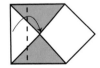

3. Fold over the left edge.

4. Mountain fold in half.

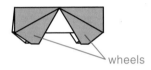

5. Fold over a little of the point.

wheels

6. With the second piece of paper, follow Steps 1–4 for making a truck.

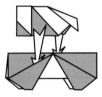

7. Insert this second piece of paper into the first, one edge on each side and behind the wheels.

BOAT

People have been using boats since prehistoric times. The oldest boat ever found is called the **Pesse** canoe and dates back to about 8000 BCE. It was dug out from a piece of pine using tools made from stone or antlers. There are many different kinds of boats. Rowboats are powered by people using oars. Sailboats are powered by the wind. Motorboats use propellers, which are powered by gasoline engines. This boat is folded from wax paper and powered by you!

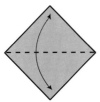

1. Use 10-inch- (25.4-cm-) square wax paper. Position the paper so that it looks like a diamond. Fold it in half, bottom corner to top corner. Unfold the paper.

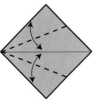

2. Valley fold the top and bottom left sides of the paper to meet at the crease. Unfold it.

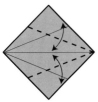

3. Valley fold the top and bottom right sides of the paper to meet at the crease. Unfold it.

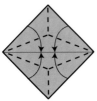

4. Valley fold the square's four edges to the center crease. The top and bottom corners will fold in half and rise in the middle. Flatten these corners to the right. Then fold them to the left.

5. Valley fold each of the flattened corners over, one to the top corner and the other to the bottom corner.

6. Flip over the two triangle shapes, left to right, and then flatten them.

7. Valley fold the top and bottom corners to meet at the center of the paper.

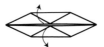

8. Open the paper in the middle and turn the paper inside out, forming the boat.

RACING BOAT

To make this boat move, you will need a large bowl of water, a few drops of liquid soap, and a few racing boats folded from wax paper. Still water has a layer of water **molecules** lined up to form **surface tension**, or a kind of skin. Soap can destroy the structure of this skin because the water molecules want to bond to the soap. Place a small drop of soap in the slit at the middle of the boat. The racing boat should suddenly race over the surface of the water. As the water pulls the soap out of the slit, it causes the boat to move in the opposite direction of the moving soap.

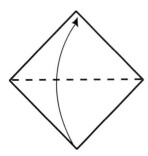

1. Use a piece of wax paper that is 8 1/2 inches (21.6 cm) square. Position the paper so that it looks like a diamond. Fold in half, bottom corner to top corner. Unfold.

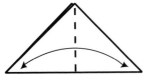

2. Valley fold in half, left corner to right corner, and unfold.

3. Valley fold the left and the right edges of the triangle to meet the middle at the crease.

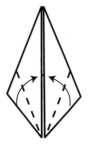

4. Valley fold the bottom left and the bottom right edges.

5. Unfold the two edges just a bit, to open the shape a little.

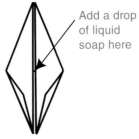

Add a drop of liquid soap here

6. Float the boat in a large bowl of water. Using a toothpick or small stick, place a drop of liquid dish soap in the middle of the boat where the slit begins. The boat should suddenly move around as if powered by a motor.

SAILBOAT

Sailboats move through the water best when the sailor moves the sail perfectly. The sailor steers the boat using sails and a rudder, a movable blade that sticks into the water. The sailor holds a rope to bring the sail closer to the center of the boat or to let it out farther. The front sail is sometimes called the jib. The rear sail is sometimes larger and is often called the mainsail. This origami sailboat is fun to sail along a smooth tabletop. You can have races with your friends' boats. Blow gently enough to move the boat without tipping it over.

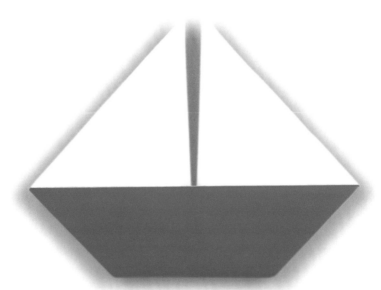

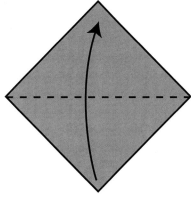

1. Use a square piece of paper 8 inches (20.3 cm) wide or less. If you are using origami paper, start with the colored side up. Fold in half, corner to corner, to make a triangle.

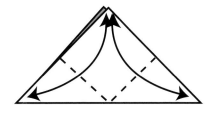

2. Fold up the left and right corners to meet at the top. Unfold.

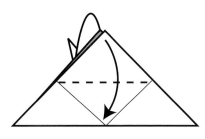

3. Fold down the two top corners, one to the front and one to the back.

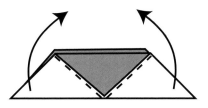

4. Fold up the left and right corners.

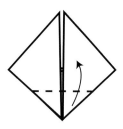

5. Fold up the bottom corner so that the tip touches the center of the paper.

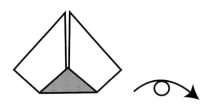

6. Turn over the paper.

SAILBOAT ENVELOPE

An envelope is also a kind of vehicle. It carries a message. Envelopes travel all over the world with the help of trucks, trains, boats, and airplanes. An envelope is a vehicle that you can use to send something special to someone in another part of the world. Although you can call people on the telephone or email them your message using a computer, these messages are not as personal or as unique as a letter mailed in an envelope you made yourself. This clever design holds itself together without glue or tape. You can make this sailboat envelope as large or as small as you need. Now you can send your best wishes to a friend by way of a sailboat!

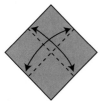

1. Use a square piece of paper 8 inches (20.3 cm) wide or more. If you are using origami paper, start with the colored side up. Fold in half, edge to edge, both ways to make crossing creases.

2. Carefully fold the bottom corner to the center where the creases cross. Unfold. Turn over the paper.

3. Fold the bottom right edge to the crease, then unfold. Repeat with the bottom left edge.

4. Fold up the bottom corner to touch the crossing creases. Fold in the left and right corners to line up with their creases.

5. Fold up the bottom edge. At the same time, fold in the left and the right edges. Make each end of the mountain fold meet at the center of the paper. Look at the next picture to see what the paper should look like.

6. Mountain fold the top and the bottom corners to the back. Turn over the paper.

7. Fold down the top edge. Make the paper fold at the top of the white triangle. Put your letter or card behind the white triangle when using this envelope.

8. Fold in the sides and tuck them behind the sailboat. The envelope locks itself closed!

DUCK BOAT

This origami model is called the duck boat because it is half duck and half boat. It is made to float on water. To prevent your duck boat from getting wet, fold it with wax paper. Paper coated with wax is waterproof. You can also color a piece of paper on both sides with crayon to waterproof the paper. Fold neatly so that your duck will balance on water. Open both wings so that the bottom of the duck is wide and flat. Place your duck boat on water and make it sail by blowing on it. Have duck boat races on the water with your friends.

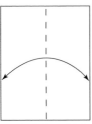

1. Use an 8 1/2-by-11-inch (21.6-x-27.9-cm) paper. Valley fold the paper in half lengthwise. Unfold.

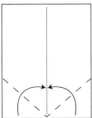

2. Valley fold the corners of the bottom edge so that they meet at the center crease line.

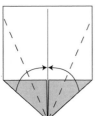

3. Valley fold the two angled edges of the folded paper to meet the center crease line.

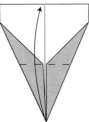

4. Valley fold up the bottom point so that it meets the middle of the top edge.

5. Valley fold down the top point so that it meets the bottom edge.

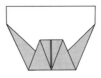

6. Turn the paper over.

7. Valley fold the paper in half. Rotate, or turn, the paper to the position shown in Step 8.

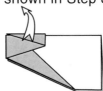

8. Pull up the neck part of the bird and flatten it to keep it in place. Look below for the shape.

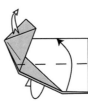

9. Pull up the beak and flatten it. Valley fold the side facing you to meet the top edge. Mountain fold the other side.

SUBMARINE

Vehicles are used to carry people and things. The submarine is a special vehicle that allows people to explore the world's oceans. Although boats and ships can travel on top of the water, storms can make this dangerous. The submarine allows people to travel deep beneath the stormy sea. When you travel on a boat, you must bring food and fresh water. When you travel on a submarine, you also need to bring fresh air or a way to purify the air you breathe. Submarines can be large or small. Some are only big enough to hold one person. Some are used to study animals that live only in the deepest parts of the oceans.

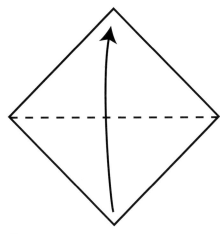

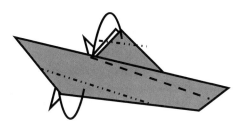

3. Fold down the back corner. Then fold the top and bottom corners to the back.

1. Use a square piece of paper 10 inches (25.4 cm) wide or less. If you are using origami paper, start with the white side up. Fold in half, from one corner to the other.

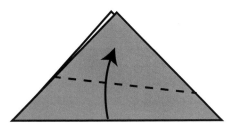

2. Fold up the bottom edge of the paper. Make one end lower than the other. The low end is the back of the submarine.

ART DECO WING

Art deco is an art style that was popular in the 1920s and the 1930s. Clean lines and simple shapes are some characteristics of art deco. This paper model is named the art deco wing because the design is simple and modern. This wing has a very low angle of **descent** in flight. This means that it will glide almost level with the ground and stay in the air much longer than a plane with a higher angle of descent. This plane is a good stunt plane, too. Throw it with extra force to make it do loops!

1. Use 8 1/2-inch- (21.6-cm-) square paper. Valley fold to make a triangle shape. Valley fold the two side corners up to the top corner.

2. One at a time, open each of the two corners to form a cone shape. Next flatten each cone shape so that it looks like a kite shape. Turn the plane over. Look at Step 3 to see how it should appear.

3. Valley fold the top corner to the dotted line. Look at Step 4 to see how your plane should appear.

4. Valley fold the remaining top corner and slip it inside the pocket you made in Step 3. Valley fold the bottom corner so that the point meets the top fold.

5. Valley fold the bottom at the dotted line. Fold each corner at the dotted line. Unfold.

6. Valley fold the two bottom corners so that the edges meet the horizontal, folded edge.

7. Mountain fold and slip the front layer in the center into the pocket you made in Step 3.

8. Fold down the folded edge. The left and right corners will move toward each other. Flatten the paper by pushing the folded edges closest to you so they line up with the edge.

9. Tuck the X tab into the nose pocket you made in Step 3.

10. Mountain fold each of the two corner layers around to the other side of the paper. Turn the wing over and let it fly!

STACKING WINGS

This origami project will show you why some paper planes fly farther than others. It has to do with the plane's shape and resistance. Take two sheets of paper the same size. Throw one into the air. Crumple the other sheet into a ball and throw it. The crumpled paper travels farther because it is **denser** and has less air resistance. Fold a stacking wing and you will see that the tail has only one paper layer but the front has many layers. The front is denser than the tail. This means that the front will have less resistance in the air than the tail. Fly one stacking wing and see how it flies. Next stack several stacking wings one inside another and see how far they fly!

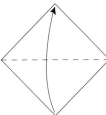

1. Use an 8-inch (20.3-cm) square paper. Position the paper so that it looks like a diamond shape. Valley fold. You will have a triangle shape as shown in the next step.

2. Carefully take the left and right ends of the triangle and valley fold so that they meet up at the center corner. Unfold.

3. Look at the dotted line above for guidance. Valley fold the first layer of the top corner. The drawing below shows how it will look after you do this fold.

4. Carefully valley fold, and slip the two side corners behind the center folded corner. If you have done this correctly, you will have made a pocket! Look at Step 5 to see how the shape should look after you have done this step.

5. Fold the left and right side corners so that they meet at the center.

6. Turn the stacking wing over.

7. Fold in half lengthwise, edge to edge. Fold so that all your folds are on the outside.

8. Open the stacking wing and flatten. Throw the wing into the air and watch it fly high over your head.

SAFE-T DART

Leonardo da Vinci (1452–1519) was a famous Italian artist and inventor. Many people believe he created the first paper airplane. Leonardo's work still inspires people today. For instance, most people have folded a paper dart airplane by the time they enter grade school. This is one of Leonardo da Vinci's designs. You can invent, too! You can fold the wings to make a different shape or you can add folded fins. This origami airplane is a **variation** of Leonardo's paper airplane. Unlike his paper airplane, this model does not have a sharp point, which can hurt someone's eye. That is why this airplane is called the Safe-T Dart.

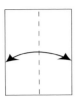

1. Start with an 8 1/2-by-11-inch (21.6-x-27.9-cm) paper. Valley fold the paper in half lengthwise. Unfold. You made a center crease line.

2. Valley fold the bottom corners to the center crease line. The bottom part of the plane should look like a triangle as shown below in Step 3.

3. Valley fold the sharp triangle point to the two center corners. This fold is what makes the plane a Safe-T Dart.

4. Study the slanted dotted lines before you fold. After you are done with this step, the two folded corners should meet at the center crease line.

5. Your plane should look like the above. The next step is to fold the plane lengthwise along the center crease. The folds of the paper should be outside.

6. Turn the plane so that the Safe-T Dart's nose is facing left. Make sure the open part of the plane is facing upward. Valley fold the side that is facing you, and mountain fold the other side.

Back view of wings

7. Open the two wings. Your Safe-T Dart should look like the above drawing from the back view. Now see how far your plane can fly!

GLOSSARY

atmosphere—The layer of gases that surrounds an object in space. On Earth, this layer is air.

bank—To turn in flight by lowering one wing.

canard wings—Wings mounted on the front end of an airplane.

compound—Two or more things combined.

denser—More closely packed together or thicker.

descend—To travel downward.

descent—Downward motion.

efficient—Done in the quickest, best way possible.

function—Use or purpose.

fuselage—An aircraft's body, not including the wings or the tail.

gliders—Aircraft that fly without a motor.

molecules—The smallest bits of matter before they get broken down into their basic parts.

Pesse—A village in the Netherlands where the oldest boat in the world was found.

propellers—Paddlelike parts on an object that spin to move the object forward.

proportions—The measure of one part compared to another.

propulsion—The force that moves something.

stall—To come to a stop.

surface tension—The force that holds the surface of a liquid together.

variation—A different version of something.

FURTHER READING

Gillespie, Katie. *Cars, Boats, and Airplanes* (Learn to Fold Origami). New York, NY: Av2, 2014.

Montroll, John. *Batman Origami: Amazing Folding Projects Featuring the Dark Knight*. Minneapolis, MN: Capstone Press, 2015.

Montroll, John. *Superman Origami: Amazing Folding Projects Featuring the Man of Steel*. Minneapolis, MN: Capstone Press, 2015.

Montroll, John. *Wonder Woman Origami: Amazing Folding Projects Featuring the Warrior Princess*. Minneapolis, MN: Capstone Press, 2015.

INDEX